My Journey

Shelvie Hutchinson Smith

With
Carolyn Reeves

My Journey

ISBN 978-1-941512-01-2

Copyright © 2013 by Shelvie Hutchinson Smith

Published by
>	Master Design Publishing
>	789 State Route 94 E
>	Fulton, KY 42041
>	www.MasterDesign.org

All unmarked Scripture quotations are taken from the King James Version of the Bible, part of the public domain.

All rights reserved. No part of this publication may be reproduced, stored in a retrieval system or transmitted in any way by any means, electronic, mechanical, photocopy, recording or otherwise, without the prior permission of the author, except as provided by USA and international copyright law.

Printed in the USA by Bethany Press International.

Testimonials

"Seldom in life are we privileged to know someone who permeates the very presence and essence of Christ so strongly that when you are with them, His Peace comes over you like a warm fragrant bath. Well, I have had the honor. Shelvie Hutchinson is one of those precious few.

"By observing her patience in dealing with the intense emotional and physical pain she has endured, I am assured of God's unfailing grace to sustain His children during troubled times. I have watched her walk before God blamelessly, humbly, in newness of life, by faith not sight, in love, worthy of the Lord, and in truth.

"Shelvie has experienced firsthand the victory that has overcome the world, her faith in Jesus Christ. The genuineness of her faith is overwhelming and has certainly been a source of strength for me and I know she has truly walked with God."

— Dianne Davidson

"Once in a lifetime, if we are blessed, we meet someone like Shelvie Hutchinson. It is even more rare when that person becomes our friend, our mentor, our big sister, or all of the above.

"When I first met Shelvie in 1987, I was a young mom in desperate need of discipling. Shelvie first entered my life as my Sunday School teacher, but what she taught me wasn't confined to a church building. She taught me about life and loving God unconditionally. She taught me about spiritual warfare and surviving heartbreak. She modeled for me what I wanted to become—a woman after God's own heart.

"Shelvie's "salt and light" gave me a passion to minister, to teach, to write, to council women through crisis pregnancy centers and simply hunger and thirst more for Jesus. God's providential hand brought Shelvie into my life, those twenty plus years ago. God knew I needed her, for without her investment in my life, I would not be in ministry today.

"The book of Job says that in all of Job's sufferings, he never once said anything against God. He simply accepted his losses and blindly lived out his faith. I've often thought that Shelvie's life mirrored that of Job. I have seen her survive seemingly insurmountable tragedies, yet never once heard her blame or get mad at God. How could anyone possibly live through such pain and still have peace and joy? The only explanation is Jesus.

"Shelvie has chosen faith over fear and victory over victimization. She has become a beautiful reflection of Christ to all who know and love her. I have often thought that her valuable words of wisdom could fill a book. Now they do. May you be blessed as you read them for yourself."

"God can do anything, far more than you could ever imagine or request in your wildest dreams." Paraphrase of Ephesians 3:20

— Bridgett Taylor
Bridgett Taylor Ministries

"When I first met Shelvie, I was a young single Christian. I had been reared in a great Christian family and had been under Biblical teaching my whole life. I remembered some difficult childhood events, but couldn't seem to really put my finger on what kept me from feeling peace in my life. Everyday was a struggle, a search for something. I poured over Christian books, obtaining lots of knowledge, but not finding the balm my soul needed.

"As a last effort, I met Shelvie. She shared her story with me and sent me back with homework…Excuse me? Quote specific Bible verse? Out loud? And to myself? Hmmm…

"This seemed very elementary after all my years of effort. I did not tell her I thought it was ridiculous, but I did try it! What did I have to lose? After hearing the verses over and over, God's truth penetrated deep in my soul. For the Word of God is alive and active, sharper than a double-edged sword. It penetrated even to the dividing of soul and spirit (Hebrews 4:12). I gradually began to feel hope, to feel like each day was lived with accomplishment and not defeat.

"As my soul gradually healed, my spirit began to feel prosperous and to feel God's goodness. It is a good thing to know God's Word. It is a great thing to feel it and to see that it is alive in our daily life.

"Thank you, Shelvie, for being used by God in so many lives. I love you, my friend."

— E.

"I was blessed to become acquainted with Shelvie soon after she moved to Oxford. People were drawn to Shelvie because of her pleasant nature and outward beauty; however, it was her inward godliness that was the real quality that drew others to her.

"When I met Shelvie, she seemed to be a woman who had it all. She was attractive with a loving husband and two sons. Her home was immaculate and decorated tastefully. She loved the Lord and there was no doubt that He was first in her life. There was no evidence that anything unpleasant had ever happened to her. When I was made aware of her past, it amazed me that she could have gone through such trials and still be so joyful. Shelvie truly lives Nehemiah 8:10: The joy of the Lord is my strength.

"This book is one that you will want to read over and over as your life changes. It helps us to know how others have gone through trials and tribulations that they did not cause, but that God allowed and used to glorify Him.

"I had the privilege of walking closely with Shelvie through the death of her two precious sons and her husband. She amazed me with her ability to mourn with grace and continue to trust her faithful God to sustain her. He not only sustained her, but He gave her hope and joy. I saw Shelvie cling to God's Word and claim it in the midst of her storms. As you read the book, you too will be encouraged to cling to God, because you will understand that is the only way to have real joy.

"Her example has caused my relationship with the Lord to be so much stronger. How thankful I am for my friend and that she has chosen to share her life lessons with others through this book."

— Pat McDaniel,
Director, Ladies Prayer Ministry
at North Oxford Baptist Church

Dedication

To the memories of my family with gratitude for their love:

To Jim for being a godly loving husband and father

To Jimbo, God's gift to us, for the bond of love we had and the things we shared

To Jeff, a strong young man who taught me much, for the love and respect we shared

To Mother, a great woman of faith, for her strong love that she gave to me and her children

To Douglas for the love, respect, and encouragement he always gave me

To Neal for the bond we had together

Acknowledgements

To my husband Smitty for his encouragement.

To many of my family and friends for their prayers for me.

Especially to our Lord Jesus Christ for His eternal love.

Contents

Preface

1. Beginning the Journey 1
2. Life Suddenly Changes 5
3. Born Again 9
4. Becoming a Wife and Mother 13
5. Entering the Valley of the Shadow of Death 19
6. Engulfed by Darkness 25
7. Searching for Help 29
8. Breaks in the Storm 33
9. Healing 37
10. The Losses Restored 41
11. Jim's Battles and Victories 45
12. Our New Life in Oxford 51
13. Strength for the Future 55
14. Jimbo 57

15	Jeff	61
16	Jim	65
17	Losing Jeff	67
18	From Oxford Back to Aiken	71
19	Life in Aiken	75
20	Losing Jimbo	79
21	Douglas	83
22	Losing Jim	86
Epilogue		93
Spiritual Victory		95

Preface

The Old Testament book of Ruth gives an account of the life of a woman named Naomi. She moved from Bethlehem to Moab with her husband and two sons for a while, because of a drought. They adapted to their new country and her sons married women from Moab. Then her husband died and both of the sons also died.

With her family gone, Naomi decided to return to Bethlehem. One of her daughters-in-law, Ruth, insisted on returning and staying with her and accepting the God and people of Naomi as her own.

When Naomi returned to Bethlehem, she tells the townspeople not to call her "Naomi", which means pleasant, because her life had been made bitter. But this was not how the story ended. Through God's grace, a kinsman redeemer married Ruth, and Naomi's family was restored. Years later her great grandson, David, became the King of Israel through whose lineage Jesus was born.

After a series of great losses and disappointments, Naomi's life and family were restored. She again was called Naomi, because her life became abundantly pleasant and satisfying. Even more, Naomi's life was recorded in Scripture, with a role in God's plan for redemption and salvation through Jesus.

This book is the story of another woman who was not defeated by a two-year battle with severe depression and the loss of her two sons and her husband. Shelvie Hutchinson transparently reveals how she first dealt with a period of severe depression and then later dealt with a period of crushing grief.

However, this is not a book about martyrdom, just getting by, or even suffering bravely. It is about overcoming tragedies and losses and still living a pleasant, God-honoring, victorious life. It's about receiving true healing from depression and replacing grief with hope through God's grace. Ultimately, it is about sharing a living hope with others.

Shelvie doesn't look back at her life's journey with bitterness and anguish. She has learned what it means to wait on the Lord and receive renewed strength; to walk and run and not be overcome by weariness; and to mount up with wings of eagles and see life from an eternal perspective.

"Even the youths shall faint and be weary, the young men shall utterly fall: But they that wait upon the LORD shall renew their strength; they shall mount up with wings as eagles; they shall run, and not be weary; and they shall walk, and not faint." (Isaiah 40:30-31)

Chapter 1

Beginning the Journey

Even today I have many happy memories of growing up with my parents and younger brother and later a baby sister in small Georgia towns. My attractive mother was hard-working, efficient, and thrifty. Daddy worked hard, but he had a way of making work seem like fun to us kids.

I had a good relationship with both of my parents, but I loved spending time with my father. He was so full of life, and fun to be with. He delighted me with special treats and hugs and often let me tag along as he ran errands. We had many good times together. There was a feeling of security when he was around, and I was always confident of his love for me.

My parents loved all of their children, and they loved each other and got along well except for one thing. Daddy loved to gamble. I thought he was the best father in the world, but as I grew older, he was away from home more and more. His occupation shifted from farming to gambling and operating a night club.

Daddy opened the night club over Mother's strong protests. For a while, his business was financially a good source of income. Daddy knew how to make his customers have a good time and want to come back.

Still, nothing in those early years could have prepared me for the disaster that was about to send Daddy to prison, plunge us into poverty, and leave me vulnerable to an intense battle with depression years later. Nor could I have foreseen that further down the road there would be a period of deep grief.

My desire in writing about the difficulties in my life is simply to share some of God's provisions for dealing with life's trials. I have attempted to include both the wrong things that prolonged the difficulties and the right things that eventually led to victory. I realize that many family members, friends, and acquaintances have impacted my life in both positive and negative ways. In absolutely no way do I intend to blame anyone for my personal problems. My reaction to the events in my life determined their impact. Surprisingly little of what happens to us in life leaves us with permanent scars and disabilities, if we respond to our problems through God's strength, grace, and wisdom.

I do not feel that my experiences were more difficult than those encountered by many other people, but they do provide a testimony that Jesus is truly The Savior and is truly sufficient for our needs. Problems and difficulties continue to present themselves, but I know that I am not facing them alone. God's grace is magnified during those times. My life today is deeply satisfying and I will be eternally grateful to God for allowing me to experience real life lived in His power.

Praise be to God, there is a Way into a Kingdom of joy, peace, and righteousness! Even when the storms do come, we can be like the builder in Jesus' parable who built his house upon a rock, and it stood firm when the winds blew and the waves beat against. (Matthew 7:24-27)

Chapter 2

Life Suddenly Changes

Everything changed for my family the night we received word that there had been an accident at Daddy's night club. A group of men had gotten into a big argument and before it was settled, one of the men had been shot. My father was held in the local jail the rest of the night. The next day came bringing the devastating news that the wounded man had died, and my father had been charged with his murder.

In the close-knit community where we lived, everyone's attention focused on this event for months. First, there was the investigation. As more details began to surface, we all felt that the charge of murder was excessive. We kept expecting the charges to be changed to manslaughter at most.

By the time that the trial began, I had convinced myself that my father could not possibly be found guilty of murder, because he was such an easy going, gentle man. He was always the peace maker when others became upset. I felt that everything was going to be all right soon. But that was not to be. As the trial finally ended, my mother had to come home and tell us that the verdict was guilty. My father had been sentenced to life in prison! I remember running from Mother out into the yard and screaming uncontrollably.

I never really said much about the trial and the sentencing from then on, but the hurt didn't go away. Every detail of the shooting and the trial had been reported on the front pages of the local paper, and the subject had dominated the conversations of the local townspeople for weeks. Even the children at school knew all about what had happened. I often had to endure overhearing conversations about my dad and even being called names by the children at school. Life went on for us, but nothing was ever the same again.

In addition to the emotional pain we all felt, the final insult was that we became victims of poverty. My mother had all she could do to support herself and her three children.

Small rural towns and churches have a legacy of quickly coming to the aid of those around them who are in need. Yet, our situation seemed to be the exception. My mother had not attended her parents' church in several years, because as a teenager, she had been instructed by church leaders not to come back until she could find dresses that were an appropriate length. "Appropriate length" for this congregation was almost ankle-length and very much out of style.

These were generous, self-sacrificing people who were glad to help anyone in need, but they stubbornly insisted that we would first have to submit to all their requirements in order to receive their financial help. Even though my grandparents were members of this congregation, we were reluctant to adapt to such a restrictive lifestyle.

There was also a strong determination on the part of the dead man's family and friends to see that adequate justice was served. When Daddy first left for prison, he was only five minutes away from where we lived. This was close enough for mother to pack a lunch and visit him every Sunday. Mother was a wonderful seamstress, and she made me several beautiful new dresses for these visits. It wasn't long until the talk of the town was that Daddy was having it too easy. After a few months he was shipped to another prison that was too far away for us to visit often.

Eventually, we lost our home and our car and were forced to move into a small apartment. At one point, we found ourselves without enough money to buy food. Mother decided to swallow her pride and ask for help from the local welfare office. She was closely questioned about how she could afford the nice dresses I wore to school. The welfare workers seemed to think Mother had a hidden supply of money she wasn't telling them about.

All they would agree to do was to allow us $40.00 a month provided Mother was not working. Our rent was $45.00 a month. Furious at their logic and lack of compassion, Mother refused their offer and took two jobs to support us for the next few months. She left home at 5:00 am and returned home at 11:00 pm, leaving me, as a twelve year old, with the responsibility of taking care of a younger brother and sister.

Mother had a difficult time providing for her family without Daddy's help, but she was determined to take care of us. We moved around several times, and Mother tried different lines of work and business ventures.

She even married again for a brief time to a fine man who provided us with a beautiful home and the things we needed. Only a few months into the marriage, he developed some strange troubling behaviors. Mother became really concerned for all of our safety and separated from him. We later found out that he had a brain tumor and died not long after Mother left.

We finally settled in Aiken, South Carolina, where Mother successfully managed boarding houses. For the first time in several years, we were living above the poverty line and did not have to worry about finances. Throughout this entire time, the only financial help we received was a $500.00 loan from Mother's brother. This allowed us some much needed relief from the pressures of long hours of working for Mother and baby-sitting for me. We were extremely grateful for his help. But for the most part, neighbors, relatives, and friends kept their distance and did little to lighten or share our difficulties.

At such a young age, not knowing how to deal with the situation we found ourselves in, I began pressing down the heartaches I felt: the unkind remarks I heard from both adults and children, the loneliness, the fears, the unresolved hurts, and all the other emotions that swirled around my life. Outwardly, I seemed to have everything under control.

Chapter 3

Born Again

When I was seventeen, my need for a place of rest and peace and predictability prompted me to move in with my mother's parents in the country and attend a small school there. I'm still not sure what kind of logic led me to do this or even why Mother gave me her permission to do so. I just knew that, in spite of their unbending strictness, they had always provided a degree of security for me. I knew that they and their home were always available for me as long as I submitted to their rules.

There was never any question about my grandparents' rule on church attendance. Church attendance took precedence over everything else, including homework and school functions. Grandpa and Grandma went to church often, with services sometimes lasting until 11:00 pm. I knew this was their rule before I moved in with them, so I didn't complain.

After a few months of all-I-could-stand church attendance, my grandmother announced that for the next two weeks we would be attending a nightly revival at another church. I did not think I could endure two straight weeks of nightly church. For the most part, church was extremely boring and unrelated to my "real" life. I wanted to announce firmly, "No. I am not going." But I knew this would be a battle I could not win. Reluctantly and resentfully, I was ready by 6:00 every night, although it really didn't matter if I was ready or not. We pulled out at 6:00 one night with my wet hair still in rollers.

Most of the sermons were of a condemning nature, and almost always included scathing denouncements of "worldly living." There was so much emphasis during church services on women not wearing make-up, not cutting their hair, and not dressing indecently, that I had come to believe that these things had a lot to do with salvation.

One night, during the revival as the invitation was being given, a man stood up and said that he felt God was calling someone in the audience and for that person to go home and read John 3:3. I couldn't wait to get home and see what this verse said. I discovered that wonderful verse says, "You must be born again." In fact I read the entire chapter of John 3 over and over again. The soft gentle words spoke deeply to my heart. They were a stark contrast to the harsh negative messages we usually heard at church.

That night God somehow managed to present the truth of His gospel to a weary young girl who was searching for peace. Even though I knew no other scriptures and had limited Bible teaching before moving in with my grandparents,

God convinced me of my need for Him and His provisions for salvation through Jesus.

A few nights later, I walked to the altar during the invitation and prayed for the Lord to let me be born again into His Kingdom. It was a sincere prayer that God heard and answered. But then a seemingly innocent remark by a lady in the congregation planted a dangerous seed of legalism. She slipped down beside me at the altar and gently suggested that the Lord would hear me if I would take off my earrings. A deep longing was satisfied that night as I came to know my Lord, but for years to come, I would have great difficulty separating "salvation through Jesus" from rules and regulations.

The next day, I wrote my mother a letter and asked her to forgive me for all the wrong things I had done in disobeying her and for my selfish attitude. I'm not sure how well I said what was really in my heart, but Mother received it exactly as I intended it. She immediately came to be with me and went with us to the revival the next night. That night Mother made a life-changing recommitment of her own to the Lord and made peace with her parents.

Everything seemed so right and wonderful that night. Then a few days later, I came home from school still wearing makeup. I usually wore no makeup around my grandparents, but saw no problem with wearing it at school. My grandmother reacted as if I had betrayed her and was living a secret life of unrestrained sin. In her anger, she accused me of many things that were not true. She continued to rebuke me to the point that I had to call Mother to come and take me home.

In spite of the battle over wearing makeup, my experience with the Lord remained genuine and continued to grow. Mother and I and the two younger children started attending a church in Aiken. This church was much less legalistic than my grandparents' church, but I still did not have the spiritual maturity to discern between the mixture of truth and error I brought with me. I knew the reality of Jesus and the salvation He provided through simple faith, but there was ongoing confusion about the "rightness" of wearing makeup, jewelry, and attractive clothes; having some of the luxuries of life; and engaging in "worldly" activities. There was also confusion about how to acknowledge sins in the lives of other Christians without being condemning and unloving.

Eventually Mother and I restored harmony with Grandma and Grandpa, but it would take a journey through a very dark valley to separate the enduring God-given truths I possessed from the man-made rules and false doctrines that were part of my belief system.

My grandparents loved their church and their Savior and had a passionate zeal for the things of God. It's ironic that the greatest blessing in my life, as well as the most destructive problems in my life, came out of that same little church.

Chapter 4

Becoming a Wife and Mother

I'm not sure when I first realized that I wanted Jim Hutchinson to be my husband. There was a strong attraction to him from the first time I saw him at the age of twelve. We both lived in the same small Georgia town and quickly became good friends. One of the highlights of our week would be walking to the Saturday afternoon movies together. Something very special was revealed about Jim as we developed our friendship in this way.

I was responsible for babysitting both my little sister and my little brother on Saturdays; so they were always along wherever I went. I'm sure we were quite a spectacle as we made our way to the movies holding hands with a slow moving toddler, and with a small boy following behind us, making all of the comments he could think of that would be embarrassing to a young girl. Jim accepted all of this with good humor and tolerance. We enjoyed each other's company many afternoons in a movie house, sandwiched between a sleeping child and a feisty little boy.

Years later, during one of our many moves, Mother decided to take us back to Georgia. Things were financially all right at first. Then things got bad again, and we moved back to Aiken. But during that brief time, something happened that was an important part of my future. I renewed a friendship with Jim Hutchinson. We were both in high school, but we were very attracted to each other and talked of marriage in the future.

After we moved back to Aiken, Jim and I kept in touch, even though we weren't able to see each other very often. Jim graduated from high school and started to college. After graduation I attended a school to become a beautician. After working for a while, I looked into the possibility of attending a nearby college and considered several other options. I prayed earnestly about what to do, but at this point Jim and I seemed to be headed in different directions.

I was making plans to attend college that fall when a letter arrived from Jim. He wanted to come over to see me. So, he drove over from Atlanta. He came again and then again until he was coming often.

I continued to talk with the Lord about what I should do. It became clear that the deep desire of my heart was to have a Christian husband and children. The only problem was that the man I was dating was not a Christian.

My Journey

I was still very attracted to Jim, but I struggled about whether or not to continue this relationship. Jim often went to church with me, but it was obvious that he did this for my benefit. I tried to share my faith with him only to realize the he wasn't really interested. It was disappointing to see that salvation through faith in Christ wasn't important to him. I finally made the difficult decision to end our relationship unless we were both in complete agreement about our Christian beliefs. I couldn't have a Christian home unless I had a Christian husband.

This was July, and the opportunities for the fall were still not settled. I remember an anguished prayer in which I told the Lord, "I love Jim and I believe he loves me, but Your Word says not to be unequally yoked together. If this is Your will, may he be saved quickly."

The next Sunday, Jim had driven over to see me, and as usual, we went to church. But something was different this time. Instead of sitting through the service bored and uninterested, he was intently listening to the pastor's words. I noticed that he was beginning to tremble as the invitation was given. Without a word, he suddenly left his seat and walked down to talk with the preacher. I watched in amazement as my prayer was answered.

Our friendship deepened that year and bonded by a genuine salvation experience in each of our lives, we decided to get married. We began our life together determined to build a Christian home.

I started married life blessed to have acquired many of my mother's amazing managerial skills and ability to handle difficult situations. I had watched her start her day at 4:30, cook breakfast for her boarders, manage the finances wisely, and confidently handle any problems that arose. I took pride in my own abilities to keep an orderly house, manage our children, and serve in our church.

Our oldest son, Jim Jr., had been born in spite of a fertility problem which my doctor had said would most likely prevent a pregnancy. Our youngest son, Jeff, was the result of many prayers and came to us through adoption. My children required a lot of wisdom and energy every day, but they were wonderful and brought us much joy. I couldn't have loved them more.

While Jim Jr. was still a baby, I gave up the financial security of my job as a beautician to stay home full time with him. This also allowed me to devote more time to the ministries of our church. We agreed this was what we should do, but eliminating my salary was a big step of faith of both of us. Jim almost immediately received a substantial raise, so there was never a financial burden on us as a result of my not working.

My faith in God seemed strong. I believe He had blessed me with a Christian husband, my children, and financial security. I had become quite comfortable and bold in sharing God's plan for salvation with others. I had also begun to discover a passion for counseling other women about how they could strengthen their homes by applying Scriptural principles.

God's presence and His Word were important parts of my life. However, I still struggled with a false view that the things I did for God were the basis for His approval for me. If I had worked hard on something at church, I felt close to God, but if I had spent too much time shopping or doing fun things for myself, I felt unworthy of God's blessings. I was even beginning to believe that the more I did for God, the greater the rewards would be. Somewhere in my spirit, I had tucked away a doubt that maybe salvation was actually Jesus plus some rules about how we dress and act.

However, a battle with depression was the last thing I ever expected to face.

Chapter 5

Entering the Valley of the Shadow of Death

Jim and I spent our first 17 years of marriage building our family and becoming part of the community and the church in Miami. I had every reason to be content and happy and enjoying life. Indeed, life was good.

Then with brutal suddenness, a terrifying period of darkness engulfed my life. It seemed to come out of nowhere, trapping me with unreasonable fears that I could not get away from. I had no idea where these strange emotions were coming from or why I was so firmly trapped by them.

Shelvie Hutchinson Smith

Even now the sudden ferocious attack of depression is baffling to me. As strange as it seems, it was related in a major way to misguided ideas about serving God and being a good person.

Just before the depression started, Jim and I had renewed our commitment to build a Christian home and support our church in Miami. Our pastor saw us as a perfect example of a Christian family, so he asked me if I would teach a ladies Bible study on how to have a Christian home and also serve as the director of the women's ministry. He felt that I should be able to help other wives strength their homes. My husband encouraged me to do this, although I wasn't so sure about taking on these responsibilities. I accepted these positions with great reluctance.

The truth was I was tired and worn out from the events of the past three years. There had been a series of problems to deal with, including a health issue and three major residential moves.

I just wanted to take some time to rest, but my religious background stressed "working hard for the Lord" and "always doing our best" and "keeping on." The equally important teachings on "the Lord's rest" and "grace" had been given little emphasis, and I had only the faintest understanding of these tremendous truths.

I did not understand that my religion consisted of that dangerous mixture of law and grace Paul so strongly warned the Galatian Christians to resist.

I did not know that God loved me as His child, in the way a father cares for his child regardless of the work that child might do for him. I did not realize that most of my religious efforts had been operating in my own strength and that my own energy and zeal had run out. I knew almost nothing about God's provisions for victory in spiritual warfare.

Through my unbalanced and distorted view, I saw God as a powerful king who demanded complete faithfulness and our best efforts; was intolerant of weaknesses or mistakes; and granted special favors only to those saints who had proven their love through great sacrifices. I felt compelled to do all I could to teach this class properly.

The class began with a large group of very supportive women who seemed to readily accept and respond to my teachings. The pastor frequently made encouraging remarks about how well I was doing in leading the class. He didn't know that preparing the lessons was becoming more and more difficult, because I had little enthusiasm for what I was teaching and little joy in my daily Christian walk.

I tried to recommit my talents to the Lord, redouble my efforts and mentally pump myself up to stimulate interest in the lessons. Still, the class, and even the church in general, was becoming more of a drudgery and a burden. I made several attempts to go to the pastor and ask him to find someone else to take over my duties, but he remained convinced that I was the one for these jobs.

Then the news came that my father had suddenly died! My father had received an early parole from prison, but he not been an integral part of our family for many years. My relationship with him was still good, but he never had a phone installed and due to the distance between us, I was seldom able to visit with him. But hearing that he was irretrievably gone left me in a state of shock.

As I made arrangements to attend his funeral, strange unexpected emotions began to surface. A mixture of love and hate rose up with such intensity, that I could hardly deal with my feelings throughout the funeral. His death exposed a multitude of repressed memories and feelings that wouldn't go away.

The week following my father's funeral was especially depressing, but I was determined to prepare for the ladies Bible class anyway. Feeling like a martyr, I made the necessary preparations for class.

As class was beginning, I opened with prayer. I was startled and shocked by an unexpected "voice" that suddenly burst into my conscious thoughts with great intensity. It was not an audible sound, but a forceful, harsh, demanding thought that said, "Why are you praying? God does not hear you." These words were as real as if someone had spoken it standing next to me. I did not know where this was coming from. It was a frightening experience and it began to produce a strange doubt about my salvation and my relationship with God.

I examined my life for areas of hidden sin and for things that might be displeasing to God. An elusive feeling of being evil, wicked, and falling short of God's standards haunted me.

Later that night as I attended church service, strange thoughts began to bombard my mind. Then I suddenly felt engulfed by a spirit of darkness and fear. I left church that night disturbed and frightened.

I rehashed that night over and over for the next few days, and came to believe that I must have displeased God by not wanting to continue teaching and leading the women in our church. I even thought that I had cut myself off from God by resisting what He had for me to do in the church. These were irrational thoughts and they were certainly not from God, but once I accepted the first irrational thought, others seemed to fall in behind it.

My Journey

I tried to reassure myself that I was just having a bad week, but there was no letup of the harsh troubling thoughts once they started. "You said no to God, and now He's through with you." "God was trying to help you and you would not listen." "You had your chance and now there is no hope." "God does not hear you—just give up." "It's too late now; you've lost your salvation."

Mixing in with this chorus were long forgotten reprimanding remarks made to me by my grandparents. I had always known that their words, even when critical, were spoken out of a concern for my well-being. Now it was as if these same words were being channeled through some cold-blooded judgmental voice, which contained absolutely no mercy. Amazingly, I accepted these harsh, unmerciful words as coming from God Himself. It would be easy for me today to recognize such thoughts as coming from the enemy, but at that time in my life, a dark cloud had shut out Truth and Light and ushered in a state of confusion.

It had only been a few weeks since my father's death. At his funeral, volumes of suppressed hurts, anger, unforgiveness, and bitterness from my childhood had been revealed and exposed. As hard as I tried, I couldn't suppress or ignore them any longer. I felt like a hurt, angry little girl again.

I probably could have dealt with the emotional problems and continued to live a seemingly normal life except for one thing: I had begun to doubt my salvation and even to believe that God found me unacceptable and unworthy of His love. With doubts about how to maintain salvation, the strange, false thoughts found an entrance to my life. They broke down all resistance and I found myself trapped in a terrifying encounter with depression.

Shelvie Hutchinson Smith

I am still amazed at the suddenness and fury of the depression that engulfed my life. Within days, a seemingly rational, stable woman was visibly becoming irrational, unstable, and deeply depressed.

Chapter 6

Engulfed by Darkness

One morning I carried my sons to school and returned alone to an empty house. Fears rose up like mighty waves, growing in intensity and bursting out everywhere. I had always taken pride in my ability to overcome fears and handle difficult situations, so being overcome by fears was a major defeat.

Once, at the age of twelve, mother was operating an apartment house. I had been left in charge of baby-sitting my younger brother and sister. A woman lived in one of the apartments, and during a bitter argument, her ex-husband shot and killed her with a single, up-close shotgun blast. After hearing the commotion, I ran into the hallway and looked straight into the apartment which contained the body of the murdered woman. From around the corner, I could hear the labored breathing of the man with the gun. Suppressing my fears, I went back to our apartment, grabbed my baby sister, got someone to call the police for help, and found my mother and bother. We then heard the second shotgun blast that signaled the suicide of the distraught husband.

A feature story appeared in an Atlanta newspaper which described the brave actions I had taken that day. I remember the sense of control and accomplishment I felt at being able to react quickly to secure the safety of my family and neighbors. I had maintained this kind of strong, capable personality all of my life. Now, for no logical reason, I was being inundated by strange, irrational fears, over which I seemed to have no control.

Then came a different kind of attack. This was confusion. I became unable to reason through anything. All decisions were difficult and some were impossible. Cooking meals became especially difficult because of the decisions involved in planning a meal. Even simple household chores became major ordeals. All of this was in stark contrast to my normal habits and character. Neither cooking, housework, nor grooming had been a major problem for me throughout our marriage, but suddenly they were transformed into giant obstacles.

Following the attacks of fear and confusion, I began to look for who or what was to blame. Accusing thoughts looked for others to blame. At times I blamed myself and even God for everything that was happening. There was massive self-pity and self-centered thoughts that would not allow me to see beyond my own problems. I thought that if things had been different, I wouldn't be in this mess.

Finally, the terrifying thought that I might have committed an unpardonable sin began to attack my sanity. I tried to read my Bible and pray to receive comfort. My prayers seemed to

My Journey

bounce off the walls. Taunting thoughts filled my mind with the idea that God wasn't listening anymore. Everything I tried to read in my Bible was blaming, accusing, and condemning.

By now I was unable to sleep and I had lost my appetite. As my physical resistance weakened, so also did my emotional, mental, and spiritual resistance. Then the poisoned thought that I was no good to anyone began to come to me. This thought was repeated over and over in my mind until I really started to believe that my family would be better off without me. Even though I knew they loved me, it seemed that if I was just out of the way, they could get on with their lives.

Unrelenting feelings of hopelessness and agony intensified, and I had thoughts of ending my life. These destructive thoughts began to cause me to lose all hope. I finally told God that I couldn't live like this any longer, and I tried to end my life. I didn't want to die and I knew that suicide was not the answer, but after weeks of sinking deeper and deeper into depression, I just wanted to find a way to end the pain. I'm so thankful that powerful prayers of others and God's mercy prevented me from succeeding.

Chapter 7

Searching for Help

Jim found my behavior as baffling as I did. He first tried to reason with me. Sometimes he would become angry when he thought I wasn't really trying to get better. This just made things worse for me. Realizing that he was not getting anywhere in trying to get to the bottom of my depression, he took me to talk with several pastors and various psychiatrists and psychologists.

One doctor focused on my low self-esteem. I certainly thought poorly of myself, but not because of any past problems with self-esteem. I felt like a failure because I had tried so hard to overcome the problems I was facing and nothing I had done had made any difference.

Another doctor wanted to treat me with massive amounts of medication. I resisted this treatment because the medication only added to the confusion and gave me no relief from the tormenting thoughts.

Visits with my pastor would bring some temporary relief, but this would vanish as soon as we left his office. These attempts only left me more frustrated and convinced that there was no hope.

One counselor focused on finding an outward "problem" and then finding a solution to whatever was wrong. He asked the usual questions: "Is your husband abusive or unfaithful? Are you involved in a controversial or immoral situation?... Are there financial problems?... Are you children in trouble?" I truthfully answered no to each question. All of the things I had really ever wanted in my life had been fulfilled.

I had a loving, supportive Christian husband and two delightful sons. I was a genuine born-again Christian, with an active leadership role in our church. We were living in a lovely new home and the job of being a full-time homemaker was very satisfying to me. There were no major outward problems in my own life or in the lives of family members that could have remotely justified my sudden decent into depression.

My church family could not understand why I couldn't just "snap out of it" and get on with my life. I could sense people losing sympathy with my struggle and moving away from me.

At times I was manipulative and deceitful with those who were trying to help me. I knew what they wanted to hear me say, and I would simply respond in that manner regardless of how I really felt.

I desperately wanted to get my life back to normal. I had done everything I knew to do. I had sought help from many places, and I had cried out to God to help me. The pain and confusion became so intense that I didn't see how even God could restore my mind.

When Christmas arrived I was at an all-time low. Jim's mother had come to live with us that winter. I don't know how we would have managed if she had not come. Determined that we would have a family Christmas, Jim and Mrs. Hutchinson and the boys decorated and did the cooking.

I went shopping with Jim, but I seemed to be in a trance-like state and made no suggestions for gifts for anyone. I remember the night the tree was brought in for decoration. I wanted to do something for the children's sake but I just couldn't. I anxiously held an ornament in my hand for hours unable to find a place for it.

The depression had begun in October and by the end of February, there had been almost no let up. Almost everything I had trusted in and built my life around seemed to be unraveling. Professional doctors and counselors had not been able to help. The church seemed powerless to change anything. My family was hanging in there with me, but they could do little to help me escape from the terror and torment I was experiencing.

The greatest hope came from the times when Jim would gather our family together and pray. He would often end by saying, "Someday this will be as if it had never been."

I know now that God did hear me and that He eventually provided the truths that brought me out of that terrible storm of depression and darkness. Moreover, He restored all that was lost during the storm.

Chapter 8

Breaks in the Storm

As spring began, there was a break in the depression. Jim was listening to a Christian radio station one day and heard a local Christian psychiatrist speaking. He was impressed with the doctor's Bible-based treatment and common sense approach. Jim immediately called the doctor's office and set up an appointment for me to see him.

I thought this was just going to be another futile session that would waste everyone's time. I went with great reluctance, but it provided me with the first ray of hope that I had had in months.

Dr. B began by praying and binding Satan. We talked about what was going on. His response was cautious, but to me it was tremendously comforting because it pointed to a cause and that cause wasn't God. "You're under a severe satanic attack, but I do believe there may be hope for you."

I reluctantly continued the sessions with Dr. B, although my progress seemed painfully slow and frustrating at first. I was embarrassed to have others know that I was seeing a psychiatrist. But, Jim was both encouraging and insistent that I follow through.

Eventually Dr. B helped me to recognize the suppressed thoughts and emotions in my life. Once they were brought into the light, I began to submit them to God and allow Him to help me deal with them. There were feelings of fear, bitterness, anger, hate, and unforgiveness, which I had effectively pushed into my subconscious.

I thought that Christians weren't ever supposed to have these kinds of feelings, so I just pretended they weren't a part of my life. When I finally began to recognize their reality and intensity, I prayed a simple prayer and asked God to replace the hate in my life with His love. I'm not sure when I got around to forgiving everyone that I harbored bitter feelings against, but I don't know of a single person today whose memory elicits anger or hatred.

As powerful as hate was in my life, love has proven to be even more powerful. Moreover, God's love was healing. The more I forgave and loved others, the more healing I received.

I experienced a tremendous sense of peace after coming to the place of completely forgiving my father, even though he had already died. I am now able to remember the good things about my father and my childhood without any resentment or pain.

It was during the third month of meeting with Dr. B that I learned an important truth which I was able to apply a few

My Journey

days later to achieve an important victory. Dr. B always began each session with a prayer to bind Satan. He also referred to "satanic attack" on several occasions before he realized that I had absolutely no idea what he was taking about.

He explained that many of our battles are not against people or circumstances, but against a real devil, and we are wise to recognize our enemy. I commented that I must be the most ignorant Christian in the world, but he assured me that 90% of the Christians today don't understand their enemy or know how to respond to his attacks.

After this session, a long-forgotten verse began to re-emerge and kindle a seed of faith. Luke 10:19 seemed to have a message directed toward me. I found myself frequently pondering the strange words of Jesus, "I have given you authority to trample on snakes and scorpions, and to overcome all the power of the enemy; nothing will harm you." I really didn't understand at that time the importance of taking the authority that God has given His children to stand against Satan.

The sessions with Dr. B had given me hope, but the same old battles returned day after day. At times I would feel that God was still with me and would help me. Then a discouraging voice would tell me that I was a failure, that I was no good, and my family would be better off without me. These thoughts would go back and forth.

Then one day I stood in front of a mirror staring at a woman, 5 feet 6 inches, weighing 98 pounds, and looking like someone in a concentration camp. It was suddenly clear to me that I was in a life and death battle with a real enemy. I recalled the prayers and counsel of Dr. B about satanic attack. I remembered the words of Jesus and the authority He gave His disciples over their enemies. I felt anger, strength and faith rising up, as I heard myself saying, "Satan, you will not have my life. What little breath I have I will give it to God to serve Him." Several days passed before I realized that the hopeless, suicidal thoughts were gone. They never returned.

Chapter 9

Healing

Summer began with a definite improvement over my winter darkness. I was no longer living in hopelessness, but I continued to experience a level of confusion and depression on a daily basis. I was managing to keep our house satisfactorily, serve meals, keep myself neat, and help the boys with homework and school activities, but there was little joy or pleasure in anything I did.

Late that summer, Jim decided to include a visit with Mother and my stepfather in our vacation. After years as a single mom, Mother had met and married a wonderful Christian man and they now had a young child together.

That week was to provide another major victory, even though I reached a near-breaking point first. From the moment we arrived at Mother's, confusion seemed to dominate everything

I tried to do. As hard as I tried, I just could not function normally and maintain order around me. I was determined to relax and enjoy our visit with Mother and make the time pleasant for Jim and the boys, but the harder I tried, the worse I became. Each day by bedtime, confusion had become chaos. I could feel the progress I had made slipping away as depression and hopelessness tried to push back into my life.

One night in a state of near-hysteria I poured out my feelings to Mother. I told her how awful my life had become and how I wished I had never been born. Mother listened calmly as I vented a flood of emotions, fears, and frustrations. When I was finally calm enough to listen, she told me she had heard of a Christian counseling ministry that she felt could help me. She suggested that I visit one of their counselors the next day.

My stepfather and Jim were skeptical, but finally we decided that it wouldn't hurt to go and spend a day there to see what they could do. Mother set up an appointment and we left very early the next day, driving 150 miles to our destination.

Throughout the long drive, my thoughts vacillated between hopelessness and hope: "It won't help. Nothing will help. I will be in darkness and despair until I die." Then I would think, "God is still with me. He will not let me stay in this darkness forever." Little did I realize that a decisive, amazing victory was waiting for me.

My counselor was a warm, pleasant, middle-aged woman who had been through a severe bout with depression several years before. I told her that I had seen some doctors, but most of them had not been able to help me. I told her that with the help of a Christian psychiatrist I had made some progress, but depression, confusion, and fears were still robbing me of joy and fulfillment.

She quietly listened, and I realized that she understood exactly how I felt. I also sensed that she knew the way out, because she had walked this same pathway before. She offered almost no advice, but she was absolutely confident that I would be healed. Her confidence was not based on any abilities she possessed, but on an uncomplicated trust in our Heavenly Father's provisions.

She placed my head between her hands and began to pray. Her words reflected an intimate knowledge of God's sovereignty, love, power, and grace. At times she quietly praised God, and at times there seemed to be an intense spiritual warfare going on. She prayed specifically for my fears and my unbelief, for freedom and healing. Later she was joined by another counselor, who, with my mother and sister-in-law, quietly prayed for me from the back of the room.

I began to remember the many prayers of my husband and family, pastors, friends, and numerous people from all over who had lifted me up to God. My own faith began to be revived as I acknowledged God's love and power and faithfulness. Every prayer that had ever been offered to God on my behalf joined together that day, and God brought a large measure of healing and deliverance.

There was no instantaneous feeling of release, but I knew there had been a decisive victory over the depression. Great rays of God's warmth and light began to break through the darkness over the next week. The storm gradually diminished throughout that fall and winter as I discovered and rediscovered tremendous truths about God's provision for His children.

Chapter 10

The Losses Restored

*I*mprovements in my physical, mental, and emotional health were steady from that day on. There were never again periods of sliding backwards into pits of despair or hopelessness, although a mildly depressed state of mind lingered at times during that fall and winter. The difference was that I now expected full and total healing.

I was once again able to read my Bible without feeling condemned and worthless. Every few weeks, I would find a particular passage of Scripture that would bring great encouragement and strength. Three of the Scriptures that became anchors for my life were Isaiah 9:6, John 10:10 and John 15:7. I found in Isaiah that one of the Lord's names is Counselor. I realized that God would know better than anyone what I needed and that He would provide for my needs—whether through a Christian counselor or through His Word.

John told me that Satan is the one who comes to rob us of joy and blessings and that Jesus is the one who came to bring me abundant life (here and now). "The thief comes only to steal and kill and destroy; I have come that they may have life, and have it to the full." (John 10:10)

John also showed me that if His Words abide in me (not man-made rules or traditions), they would lead me into the path of freedom. "If you abide in me, and my word abides in you whatever you ask I will do." (John 15:7). I desperately desired to be completely healed and restored. This meant I was to hide and rest everything in Him. Because His Word was in me, I would know how to think and live the way Christ would have me to.

I came to settle once for all the truth that salvation and a right relationship with God is through Jesus alone—not through Jesus plus something else. God established the truth in my heart that He loves me eternally as His very own child, regardless of any sins I might commit or any failure in my life. I learned that corrections, and even chastisement, were expressions of God's love and were not meant to harm me.

The lie that had made me so vulnerable to this deception was exposed as legalism. In the past there were times when I doubted my salvation. I vacillated between trusting my own good deeds and trusting the righteousness provided by the Lord Jesus.

The depression would have dissipated much sooner if these simple truths had been unwaveringly claimed back at the beginning. My salvation had been genuine, but false beliefs planted at the same time had caused me to trust in my own self-righteousness as a means of earning God's favor.

If anyone had suggested that I were a legalistic person, I would have sincerely and emphatically denied it, even though legalism permeated my religious beliefs. I have found legalism to be one of the most deceitful and difficult heresies to recognize and find freedom from.

The difficulty in recognizing legalism as an error arises from the fine line of separation between righteousness and obedience. True righteousness can only come from faith in the sinless Son of God and is 100% grace. Legalism is an attempt to achieve righteousness with God by obeying a set of rules. Laws and rules can show us that we are sinners, but they do not have the power to change us into righteous people.

While obedience does not make us more acceptable to God, obedience to God's Word is important to a Christian. A Christian's new nature has a deep desire to please and obey God. More than anything, obedience helps us to experience a victorious, joyful life.

As winter gave way to spring, the bondage of bitterness and legalism was giving way to grace and freedom. Day by day I was regaining the ground that had been lost to the enemy during the past year and a half. In the process, lies, heresies, and false doctrines were being separated and discarded.

I had a new appreciation for the beautiful spring flowers that appeared in my yard. They seemed to parallel the return of normal pleasures in my own life. I began to bring some of my flowers in to add color to the house. After months of insomnia and irregular sleeping, I began to sleep peacefully through the night.

During the worse days of my depression, I had come to detest food and had quickly lost about 40 pounds. None of my clothes fit, but I could not bear to go shopping for new ones. I had simply pinned a few of my most comfortable clothes along the seams as carefully as I could until they somewhat fit. Now my appetite was returning and I was beginning to gain a little weight. I had also resumed going to a hairdresser occasionally for a fresh hair style. These changes were as much a relief to my husband as they were to me.

Chapter 11

Jim's Battles and Victories

Throughout that year and a half, Jim had gone through an emotional roller coaster of his own. Beginning with the initial shock of returning from a regular business trip to discover an irrational wife, Jim had fought his own personal battles. At the low points, his emotions ranged from disbelief and denial to anger and rage. As the extra burdens and responsibilities became almost too heavy to bear, he would cry out to God at the unfairness of it all.

Sometimes he would speak to me in frustrated anger, as if he were trying to force a return to normal by the sheer strength of his will. Actually, his anger was a stumbling block.

As I would try to focus on and respond to his words, I would find myself unable to be what he wanted of me. My frustration would shoot up along with a new cycle of fears, confusion, and self-hatred.

Jim finally came to believe that the boys and I could handle this better if he were out of the way. The situation became unbearable for him one night. Furious at me for not trying harder and angry at God for allowing this to happen, he quickly packed his bags to leave for good. Ignoring my tears and pleas to stay with me and the boys, he stormed out of the house.

But in one of those unique life-changing moments, God spoke to Jim. In the midst of the turmoil of that night, Jim's wedding vows were clearly and distinctly impressed upon his mind. "For better or for worse" suddenly took on a renewed commitment. To my absolute amazement, the door opened a few minutes later and a very calm and compassionate Jim stood in the room. He simple said, "We will make this together." I truly don't know how the boys and I could have made it without him.

At the high points, Jim was a tower of strength, reassuring me that I had not committed some unpardonable sin and praying for me with all the authority granted by God to a husband. Almost every night he would gather me and the boys together to pray, always praying for my healing.

The most strength and encouragement came from those times when he would tenderly affirm, "Someday this will be as if it had never happened." Today, I am able to look back at that darkness and remember what happened with no pain or anxiety. It is as if that period of depression has been cast away and a renewed life has taken its place.

Jim and I were extremely grateful to see the storm finally breaking up and to realize that we had come through the worst of it together. It seemed as if every day a small new victory was won.

But there was an unresolved point of contention that centered around an old pair of turquoise pants, carefully pinned to fit, and worn on a regular basis because they didn't have to be ironed. After a few pointed remarks about "those ugly pants," I realized that they symbolized more than an old pair of ugly pants. They represented how much the depression had robbed us of.

One beautiful spring morning, Jim came in and told me to get in the car. He was obviously taking great pleasure in what he was about to do. He was grinning mischievously as he announced, "We're going to buy some new clothes. Then we're going to burn and bury those turquoise pants."

Jim had found a dress shop in a nearby town that carried all my favorite styles. We spent the day in that little shop, while Jim bought everything I tried on and liked. Looking at myself in a full-length mirror, wearing clothes that actually fit and that were stylish, I felt like Cinderella. We returned home with a whole new wardrobe. The trip had been fun and exciting and signaled the return of an ability to enjoy life again. The hated turquoise pants were never seen again.

I'm not sure how long I was able to enjoy my new clothes, because by summer my appetite was more than normal. Every morsel I put into my mouth tasted wonderful—so wonderful in fact, that by August I had gained an additional twenty-five pounds and was back to my original weight. So many simple pleasures were re-enjoyed that summer—working my flowerbed, carrying on conversations with friends and family, enjoying the company of my husband and our sons, and laughing at jokes.

The real proof of victory over the storm came as I responded to a cluster of major difficulties. First Jim's mother died after several months of poor health. Then my stepfather was killed in a tragic car accident. I grieved over the loss of my two wonderful friends, but the depression did not return.

Jim called our pastor and a deacon to come over and pray for me when he received word of my stepfather's sudden death. They all feared that this might trigger a set-back. These same men had prayed for me months earlier at the worst time of my depression. Now they prayed again for protection and strength. I literally could feel God's strength within me throughout those days.

Within a few weeks, I had to have emergency surgery to remove a painful cyst on a kidney. This time I claimed a promise I found in Psalms that God would grant me His strength. Somewhat surprised by a rapid return of health, I left the hospital with renewed energy and a voracious appetite for food.

This new level of energy was well timed. A month later we received word we were being transferred to Oxford, Mississippi. The next week our son, Jeff, and I were turning up a long driveway with a real estate agent from Oxford. Trees formed a peaceful canopy over the driveway. Jeff commented on the number of dead trees and limbs in the huge yard that would need to be hauled out to make room for new flowers and shrubs.

I thought, "This is exactly the point where my life is now. The Lord is hauling out the rubbish in my life to make room for new growth." As Jeff continued to point out all the possibilities for beautiful gardens, my spirit grew more and more thankful for God's restoration taking place in my life.

God was not unkind when He allowed me to go through this period of darkness. At first I thought I had been abandoned in a dark valley. It was only after months of darkness that I gradually became aware of His presence, which had been with me all along. When the storm ended, a host of negative things had been swept away, preparing me for a ministry to others who feel defeated by life's hardships.

The depression never returned, even when I later went through a period of intense grief. My life was restored and the depression was completely healed. Jesus became a Living Reality in my life, and powerful Scriptural Truths became a firm foundation for me.

Chapter 12

Our New Life in Oxford

After moving to Oxford, Jim and I fell in love with its small town atmosphere and southern charm. It was such a contrast to life in the mega-metropolis of Miami. On one of our first days in town, we asked a local businessman if we could write a check for some cash. Expecting a firm denial, the smiling man surprised us by replying, "Of course." People all over town were trusting and friendly and helpful.

We quickly found a church home of wonderful Christians at North Oxford Baptist Church. Jim and I gravitated to Christian ministries soon after we moved. Jim taught a couples class for several years. I became involved in teaching Bible studies for women. I couldn't help but notice that the classes I taught were now a joy, unlike the class in Miami that had turned into a legalistic marathon.

God so blessed me by allowing me to teach groups of women, to minister as the director of the local Save-A-Life ministry, and to do some private counseling for twenty years. Oxford was the place where I saw God use the things I had suffered and experienced to help others be set free and overcome some of their difficulties.

I still occasionally meet someone whom I was able to minister to during this time. God has allowed me on several occasions to hear firsthand how their lives were turned around by something I told them years ago. Such occasions have been one of my greatest joys.

We soon developed close Christian friends who were like family. We had our share of disappointments and we had our share of wonderful blessings, but overall our years in Oxford are remembered as a period of happiness and fulfillment.

Through both disappointments and blessings, the emotional level of my own life remained amazingly stable. The Lord was my strength when I was weak, He gave me joy in good times and in bad, He gave my life purpose, and I was assured of His love and care for me and my family.

Our sons were not happy to leave old friends, but they finally settled in and found their place and made new friends. They loved the sports opportunities our church provided. They also found that our friends were like aunts and uncles to them. They came to realize they were part of a church family.

We chose the house with the long winding driveway to be our home, not realizing that its sprawling space would become a favorite hang out for many of Jimbo and Jeff's friends. There were many mornings when the phone would ring and it would be a parent checking to see if their son was still there. Boys would be sleeping all over the house, and one by one they would wake up and go home. One young man preferred to climb out the window and leave early before the rest of us woke up. Sometimes I would fix breakfast for whoever was there. They all felt comfortable there and would just make themselves at home.

We made our home a place to entertain fellow church friends. These were often spontaneous events. We also welcomed a number of visiting missionaries and pastors who were passing through. Our door was always open to young people who just wanted to talk. After they grew up and married, they often found time to come by and visit and introduce their wives.

Chapter 13

Strength for the Future

One day I read the account of the last supper Jesus had with His disciples. He knew His time of departure was near, so He set aside time to be alone with his friends for the Passover meal. After they came to the upper room, Jesus wrapped a towel around His waist and knelt beside each one and washed their feet. That night, He ministered to them on several levels and prepared them for the events that would soon unfold.

A few nights later, I sensed the Lord prompting me to get up early to pray. I quickly arose, and as I began to pray, I felt a strong presence come into my den and kneel down by my chair. I immediately knew this was Jesus. His presence overshadowed every care and concern and fulfilled every desire I could ever have.

Without hearing an audible voice, my spirit was assured that He would be my strength in the coming days, months, and years. His presence continued to be manifested to me over the next several days and to strengthen me. This was the greatest assurance of a promise I had ever experienced. At the time, I had no way of knowing how much I would need that strength in the future. I absolutely knew that whatever came into our lives, Jesus Himself held the future, cared very much about what was happening, and would sustain us through every circumstance.

For the past 40 years the Lord had led me through some difficult paths, but looking back at the past, I knew there had been purpose in where we were going. This enabled me to look to the future without fear.

Chapter 14

Jimbo

Jim Jr., better known as Jimbo, was our first-born son. We had to wait several years before I was able to conceive and finally give birth. He filled a special place in our hearts and was doted over by many relatives and friends. He grew into a tall, slim, handsome young man. His soft-spoken charm served him well in many situations.

Even as a child, he had remarkable insight and empathy for the problems of others. I wasn't surprised when he began to show an interest in studying psychology and decided to attend a Christian college after graduation.

Jim and Jeff attended a Christian school while we lived in Miami. This was an excellent school and one that was a good fit for both boys. While Jim and I were delighted in the move from Miami to Oxford, the boys had a much harder time adjusting to a larger public school. The adjustments of the move exposed insecurities in both boys. They both made poor choices in the process.

Leaving lifetime friends and trying to adjust to a new school was a stressful period for them. Jimbo left a Christian school where he was the star baseball pitcher and was accepted and well liked by other students. The culture of the school encouraged students to be considerate and helpful to others and to apply Christian principles to their lives.

Jimbo found a different kind of culture in the public schools of Oxford. Instead of being welcomed and invited to join in school functions, he felt isolated and rejected. He was even bullied and viciously teased by a group of students. Jimbo was especially teased about his tall lanky build. We noticed that he was beginning to obsess about being too thin. He finally started going to a gym where he found a new set of friends who were like-minded in their commitment to body building. It was acceptable among them to use steroids, so he decided to try them. They seemed to give him courage and confidence and helped him to quickly build up more muscles. It seemed like a perfect solution to Jimbo at the time.

After graduation from high school Jimbo spent a year at a junior college and then decided to attend Liberty University. During summer break he was the youth minister back at North Oxford Baptist Church. One of the good choices Jimbo made after coming to Oxford was to attend this church. The church teachings and activities helped to provide a network of Christian friends along with spiritual growth.

Eventually Jimbo married a young lady who also attended this church. She already had a 5- year-old, and 12 months later a beautiful granddaughter, Christin, was born. So, within a

12 month period, we had two precious grandchildren. From the beginning of their marriage finances were tight. And after 12 years of marriage the money situation had not greatly improved. Over the years other problems had formed and grown into major issues. We came to realize that another destructive factor to their marital problems was an unhealthy overuse of prescription drugs.

Eventually they made the devastating decision to end their marriage. In the divorce proceedings, Jimbo was given limited visitation rights with his children. His relationship with the children became strained and fractured. I can only say that the enemy stole that marriage and no one won in the process.

Jimbo had started working on a college degree many years earlier, but had never finished it. After the divorce he decided to finish a degree in Christian counseling with plans to be a Christian counselor. The day Jimbo graduated was a time of great celebration for us all.

Chapter 15

Jeff

Our younger son, Jeff, had a natural love and talent for growing gardens and plants. Over the years he transformed our three-acre yard into beautiful areas of rock gardens, flowered trellises, and landscaping.

Jeff was adopted at the age of 5, and he came to us with a history of neglect and an undiagnosed condition of Attention Deficit Disorder/Hyperactivity. He was happiest when he was working outside and allowed to be freely creative. He was least happy when he had to sit still inside and pay attention to someone else.

Jim expected obedience and he expected Jeff to pay attention to his instructions. Needless to say, this was difficult for a child who had an inborn problem with paying attention.

Still Jeff was an absolute delight, and I never regretted our decision to adopt him. Jeff's love for me was never in doubt. Nor did Jeff ever doubt my love for him. But his deepest feelings were kept in a locked compartment. I so wanted him to accept the complete healing that the Lord Jesus provides, but he usually kept his inner hurts and feelings of rejection hidden away inside.

Jeff enjoyed being with other people and made friends easily, but most of his friendships were somewhat casual. He only allowed a few people to get to know him at a deeper level. As he grew older, he began deal with his hurts by drinking. This became very destructive for him.

The one who became his dearest friend was Tammy. She understood and appreciated his unusual quirks and was the one he could talk to about almost anything. They spent one summer together every day, enjoying each other's company for hours at a time, sharing the same interests, and openly talking about their problems and their futures.

They even made plans to get married, but at the last minute, Jeff panicked at the thoughts of a lifetime commitment and abruptly and cruelly broke off their relationship. Tammy was heart-broken, as were Jim and I. She had already become a part of our family and was dearly loved by us all.

Jeff knew he had handled this poorly and had disappointed many people, but he didn't know how to make things right. He moved to Memphis for a few years when he was 20, and then later moved to Ft. Lauderdale. We continued to see him on friendly terms, but it was obvious he was looking for some kind of freedom from regulations and traditional ways of doing things.

His creativity and talents were best expressed through gardening and landscaping. With an eye for mixing colors and shapes, he was able to transform bare grounds into places of stunning beauty.

My children were not perfect, but they taught me so much, and I loved them both dearly. I consider myself blessed to have known the deep, absolute love and respect of the three men in my life—Jim, Jimbo, and Jeff.

Chapter 16

Jim

Jim's job required him to do minimal traveling almost every week, but he enjoyed his work and was thankful he could always be home on weekends. He provided for us well, and I didn't feel any need to look for work to supplement our income.

Jim was very athletic in high school and was an outstanding football player. His health had been good ever since I had known him. Then one day I had just returned from a long trip to visit my mother in Aiken. I walked into the house as the phone was ringing. Someone called to tell me Jim was in the hospital in Atlanta, Georgia. He had been admitted with a heart attack and was in serious condition. Jimbo immediately drove me back to Atlanta. We arrived at the hospital at 4 a.m.

Jim and I often prayed together and with a measure of faith, because so many of our prayers had been miraculously answered. The first thing Jim asked me to do when we arrive was to pray for him. Jim's condition was soon upgraded from serious to stable, and within a few days he was discharged and allowed to go home.

Over the next few years, Jim had several stints put in his heart. These were generally outpatient procedures and none of them ever had to be repaired. Each time, God graciously restored his health and he was able to return to normal activities.

In 1994, Jim's company made a number of changes in their business structure and offered Jim a generous retirement package. We felt that he was still too young to be retiring, but this seemed to be our best choice at the time. Somewhat reluctantly, we took their offer.

There were several weeks of trying to adjust to a totally new lifestyle that didn't involve getting up and going to work. Jim eventually found new interests and made a smooth transition to being a golfer and spending more time with friends and family. We even bought a small condo in Aiken so we could spend more time with our family there.

This was the same year Jeff called to tell us that he had been seeing a doctor. We learned that he was being treated for several serious conditions. Jeff put a positive spin on his condition, but we knew things had the potential to turn critical quickly. I learned later that he had a serious lung condition and spinal meninges.

Chapter 17

Losing Jeff

Jim and I had come to love Tammy even though she never got to be our daughter-in-law. We were talking one day and she mentioned a dream she had had about Jeff. In the dream she was driving her car and saw Jeff on the other side of the road. He smiled and waved to her. She felt great compassion and love for him and she wanted to go and be with him. He began to walk through the woods toward a big house and turned to tell her she could not come with him this time. As she talked, I sensed that the dream had a prophetic message in it for us all.

A short time later, we got a call that Jeff was in a hospital in Fort Lauderdale. We were told we needed to fly down to be with him, because his time might be short. We quickly made arrangements to pack our things and fly down. When Tammy heard that we were with him, she called and asked if she might come too. We were thankful to have her support.

I felt that we would be losing Jeff, in spite of hours of fasting and praying for him over the years. Even before we arrived at the hospital, the Spirit of God let me know that I would not have what I wanted with Jeff here on earth, but I would in heaven.

When we arrived at the hospital, his condition was worse than we expected. The doctor said he probably only had 5 to 7 days left. But, he was conscious, and he was glad to see us all. Many friends and family members were standing in the gap for us during those days, calling, encouraging us, and most of all praying for us. At times, I would get on my knees beside his bed to pray, but the only thing that seemed appropriate was to praise the Lord.

When Tammy arrived, Jeff's whole countenance changed and he greeted her with a big smile. We knew he could hear us, but he wasn't able to talk to us by then. She stood by his side and stroked his hair lovingly as if there had never been a problem between them.

The three of us watched Jeff leave this world, and God graciously gave us peace and strength. In our spirits, we unmistakably saw angels take him up. Jim later had a vision of Jeff entering heaven, where Jesus met him at the gate and led him over to a beautiful garden to work. I was reminded that one of my prayers for Jeff had been for him to have a home and a garden. It was not answered in the way I had hoped, but heaven took on a renewed reality that day.

It's hard to express the importance of Christian friends at a time like this. One of our friends flew down to help us drive a vehicle back and pick up Jimbo who was living in Aiken.

My Journey

Tammie and I flew back together. I so dreaded the thoughts of going back into our house and trying to get things ready for the relatives I knew would be coming soon. Jim and I had not been in our home for many days and several things had been left undone.

When we walked through the front door, I was flooded with peace and appreciation. The house was in perfect condition, and every room was clean and orderly. My thoughtful friends had carefully cleaned the house, so I wouldn't have this to worry about that chore.

Then food began to arrive, and we never had to think about preparing meals. My sister, her husband, and Jimbo arrived the next day. My church family was so kind and caring. They supported us with prayers and looked for ways to meet our physical and emotional needs. The funeral was really sweet and comforting.

I can't say that the days and weeks following was an easy time, because it was not. Grief and loss are painful. I constantly called out to Jesus for His strength and asked Him to carry me through. Jim and I clung to each other during this time and realized how much we needed each other.

Jeff's illnesses and death exposed something unexpected in Jim. He became openly angry, and was mostly angry at God. It had been hard for him to watch me suffer as Jeff made some bad decisions growing up and later as a young man on his own. It had been hard to watch Jeff lose his battle for life. But together and in unity, we continued to seek God's help. Over time Jim was able to work through his anger.

Thankfully, this was not a battle I had to fight. I suppose it was because God had let me know He was going to take Jeff home where he would be completely healed and at peace. I praised God often for this assurance. I was also very thankful for the gradual healing of the void Jeff's death left in me. God used His Word, prayers, family, friends, opportunities to serve others, and time to bring comfort.

Chapter 18

From Oxford Back to Aiken

Shortly after Jeff's funeral, we got a call from Jimbo who was back in Aiken, saying he needed help. There was urgency in his call, so we drove to South Carolina to check on him. This was when we realized his dreams for counseling and working with young people had met a huge barrier. Jimbo realized he was addicted to pain medication and knew that he would first have to deal with his own dependency before he could help anyone else. We sought out a drug rehab facility where he received treatment.

This was one of the most difficult periods of time I had ever experienced. We had one son in the grave and one son fighting to regain control of his life. Yet I was able to tell the Lord with sincerity, "You know and understand. I don't. We will just trust You."

After several months Jimbo moved back to Oxford, hoping to build a better relationship with his children, but the estrangement between them continued. He had not given up on his vision to be a Christian counselor, but the weight of his personal problems kept pulling him back.

By now my mother was living in an assisted living facility in Aiken. One of the things I most loved to do was to talk with her, which we did often. Her health was causing her some problems, but her mind was alert and she exuded spiritual wisdom. I had spent a week with her, just talking and reminding each other of God's faithfulness through some tough times. The night before I left, I found myself being the one to encourage her rather than being encouraged by her prayers and wise words.

I left early the next morning, throwing my hand out toward the building where she was staying and asking God to take care of her. Before I arrived in Oxford, she had departed this life. My husband had the sad task of telling me the news and helping me deal with the shock and grief of losing one of my dearest friends.

Again friends came and prayed with us. God gave me grace in large measure. By the next day, I was able to get up and head back to Aiken for Mother's funeral.

Her funeral was quite comforting. She was considered a spiritual rock in her community. She had also met a number of people in Oxford, who referred to her as the saint with the twinkle in her eye. As I stood by her casket, I was struck by how beautiful she was and was reminded by the Spirit that she had fought a good fight and she was faithful. Above all, she loved her Lord.

I had a chance to talk with the lady who was last with her and was thrilled to learn about her last minutes. She had gone to lunch and came back to sit down in her room. She briefly mentioned a pain in her stomach, but then she looked up and simply said, "Jesus." I realized that as I was driving home that day, she was being carried home by Jesus.

A large number of friends and relatives in and around Aiken came to Mother's funeral. This got Jim to thinking that if something happened to him, I would need to be back in that area where I would have family around me. We both loved Oxford and the friends we had there, but over the next several months this thought kept coming back to him, as God impressed John 14 and other Scriptures about moving on to heaven on his heart. When Jimbo decided to move back to Aiken, Jim felt that the time had come for us to do the same thing.

We put our house on the market and it quickly sold. We didn't say goodbye to our dear friends in Oxford. We just told them we expected them to visit us in Aiken, and we'd be coming back to Oxford again as often as we could.

Chapter 19

Life in Aiken

Jim and I joined a fine church in Aiken. Jim played golf often with a group of friends he met at church. Life was good as we were able to spend time with many former friends and family members who lived in or near Aiken—Jimbo, Jim's sister and brother-in-law, my sister and brother-in-law, my brothers, as well as a number of aunts and uncles, nieces and cousins. We were able to spend holidays, birthdays, and summer vacations together. And, friends from Oxford also came to visit.

My brother, Douglas, and I saw each other daily that first year we moved back to Aiken. We began taking long walks together to get exercise. These times were spent talking and often laughing at the crazy experiences we had as children. Douglas had been through trials and broken dreams and disappointments all his life. After a bitter divorce, he and his wife and daughters went for years with little communication.

But he was an encourager to me. He had a gift of humor and could make me laugh in almost any situation. He had a way of putting difficult memories and situations in perspective with his wit. A deep bond of friendship and brotherly love developed as we spent time together.

I'm so grateful for those years with their pleasant memories. But, Jim's thoughts about moving back to Aiken were prophetic. A few years after we moved, Jim experienced some unusual pain in his back and went to our family doctor to have blood work done. The doctor called us to come in so she could discuss the results. Our doctor and friend stood in her office with tears in her eyes as she told us she was very suspicious of one of the blood tests, so she took it on herself to send it off. The diagnosis was a form of cancer known as multiple myeloma. She gave us great hope as she laid out a plan of treatment, but also made it plain that this was going to be a tough battle.

Jim was still the picture of health. He just looked too fit to be sick. We were both shocked and we were having a hard time taking in all that she was telling us. Jim had a hard time with the diagnosis, probably much harder than I realized. But again, we sought God's strength in a spirit of unity. Gradually Jim was able to release his life and his family into God's hands.

About a year after Jim received his diagnosis of cancer, my brother, Douglas, had a near-death encounter from a massive heart attack. We received a phone call from the hospital emergency room and were advised to get there as soon as possible. In the few minutes we were able to be with him, I laid my hands on his head and prayed a bold prayer for his recovery.

His heart doctor came out to the waiting room and told us he didn't have any hope that Douglas would make it. But he defied the medical odds and was able to go home a few days later. We were even able to resume our walks.

About a year later, Douglas was diagnosed with lung cancer. Prior to this time my younger brother, Neil, had a stroke that took away much of his independence. He had moved in with my sister in a nearby town.

Chapter 20

Losing Jimbo

After several unhappy setbacks, Jimbo began to make progress in getting his life on track to be a Christian counselor. He had found a job in Aiken, and He began to do counseling three nights a week on a voluntary basis at Christ Central Ministry, a Christian center in Aiken. He had a natural gift for counseling and really looked forward to the nights when he would get to interact with people who needed help.

After his Dad got sick, Jimbo moved in with us and lived upstairs. We had everything we needed downstairs, and Jimbo was a great encouragement to his dad.

One evening as I was cooking supper, I called for Jimbo to come down and eat. When he didn't respond, I walked upstairs and found him shaking, his eyes rolled back, and unconscious. We called 911 as I raised his head and shoulders up and did what we could to revive him, all the while calling out loud to God to take care of him.

After several harrowing minutes he began to respond to us, but was very disoriented. Douglas came over and went to the hospital with Jimbo. Before leaving the paramedics checked my husband who was visibly distraught. I stayed with Jim, because I was afraid to leave him alone.

Jimbo was dismissed from the hospital the next day, but we all realized he had had a close call. The doctors determined that he had had a seizure and gave him seizure medication to take daily. Jimbo resumed counseling at the Center. I would often go with him to counsel people who came in.

On November 12 we both went in to the Center together, even though Jimbo was not feeling well that night. I noticed that he didn't look well when he took a break. I suggested that we should go on home, but he insisted that he needed to finish talking with a 16-year-old young man who had been sentenced to jail and was fearful of where he was going. Jimbo seemed determined to finish talking with him.

We stopped to get a bite to eat on the way home, but Jimbo wasn't hungry. He immediately went upstairs to go to bed, but for some reason, he came back down and gave me a big hug and said, "I love you so much." As he started upstairs, he yelled back, "I love you both."

That was the last thing he said to us. He died peacefully in his sleep. When Jim found him the next morning, he had been dead for at least a few hours.

The medics came and briefly tried to revive him, although we all knew it was too late. As they were getting ready to move Jimbo's body, I asked them to leave for a few minutes. I wanted to have some time to say goodbye and to love on my son. His face was radiant and peaceful. I knew he had left unfulfilled dreams in this life, but he had entered eternity in peace. My brother, Douglas, stayed close to me while I knelt beside Jimbo and prayed. I could feel the strength of the Holy Spirit, assuring me that He would be my strength in the days to come.

The overwhelming shock and grief seemed to be more than we could bear, but at the same time, there was abundant grace poured out on us. People from everywhere came again—family, new friends, old friends, and church friends. Friends from Mississippi, Arkansas, and Florida flew in to be with us. Jimbo's children, Christin and Landon, flew in. We were surrounded and upheld by the love of family and church and by the love of everyone who came and those who prayed for us at home. It's hard to describe what a comfort it was to have godly friends and family around or praying for us at this time.

Troy, a long time friend of Jimbo's since high school, came to preach the funeral. Troy knew Jimbo well and he was a tremendous blessing to us. Troy shared that Jimbo had been a positive influence on his life and his Christian walk. He told me and Jim how Jimbo's relationship with us had helped him learn to respect and love his own parents. Two other friends from high school came and shared some sweet memories of their friendship with Jimbo.

Several of the teens and adults Jimbo had counseled were at the funeral. They literally wept with us and mourned his death. The director of the Christ Central Ministry was heartbroken that Jimbo had been taken away, because of the impact he had on the people who came there for help.

Jimbo had been unable to have the kind of relationship he wanted with his children for the past several years. But in spite of regrets, there was reconciliation and healing as we all grieved the loss of someone we loved.

Chapter 21

Douglas

At first Jim and Douglas handled their diseases well and we were optimistic about their recovery, but as the months passed, their conditions began to worsen. There were times when I would have to take them both to the emergency room on the same day. Once, the emergency room doctor called to me through a curtain, "Shelvie, is that you?" He actually hadn't seen me. He had just recognized the perfume I usually wore.

One of Douglas's daughters, Michelle, and her husband came to stay with me during this time. They were a welcome help and just what Jim and I needed. Jim was able to go home for Christmas, but Douglas was unable to do this. I got a panicked phone call from Douglas in early January asking me to come and be with him. He knew he was dying and told me he was afraid. I prayed with him and assured him that God would not leave him and would be with him all the way. By the next day, he was calm and resolved. His daughter said she could hear him talking with Mother and telling her he was coming on home, but first he had some things to take care of.

He called again in an almost impatient manner. He said, "Shelvie, I want you to get up here now. They are waiting. You know I'm about to go to heaven." He gave me some instructions about his business to take care of and then said he would tell Jimbo and Jeff and Mother I loved them.

My last words to Douglas were to tell him how much I loved him and appreciated his encouragement. I will be forever grateful to have been available to help him during his time of sickness and to encourage him. He entered eternity a few hours after I left, surrounded by and reconciled with his daughters.

Chapter 22

Losing Jim

Jimbo's early death was traumatic for everyone, but Jim took it especially hard. From the moment he found Jimbo's body, some of his usual will to fight on was lost.

Most of the time he was able to walk around the house, but there were several times when he fell and we would have to call 911 to get him up. Once he fell in the bathtub, hurting his back and winding up in intensive care.

During this time I prayed, fasted, and called on many people and groups to pray. My sister and family, Jim's sister and family, and others were always there for me and Jim when we needed them. A lifetime friend, Bobby, was especially helpful. She had lost a son and her husband to cancer, so she knew how to comfort and encourage me.

We were upheld by friends who were praying, sending cards, calling, and helping in any way they could. Doctors did everything they could. Through and over all of this, God's strength for us was everywhere.

Jim's condition continued to worsen and he became weaker, so we were pretty much always together. For about the last year, Jim wanted me to read out loud to him from the Bible, mostly Psalms, and then we prayed for each other and for others before he went to sleep. As a part of this routine, I began to anoint him with oil as we prayed. We had called the elders to pray over him and anoint him with oil early on in his illness, but now we did this as a way of being reminded that the Holy Spirit was a reality in our situations.

When I got in bed, I always kissed him goodnight and held his hand until he went to sleep. God had given me a husband who loved me and always tried to do what was best for me for the past 52 years. Several times a day, he would pull me aside to thank me for being there with him. It was not a burden for me to minister to him.

Some days were harder than others. I would put him to bed, look back at him, then go in the living room and cry. I knew in my heart that time was short, but I kept hoping for him to be healed. Jim seemed to know he would be leaving this earth soon. Occasionally he would tell me that John 14:1-3 was for him. "Don't be concerned or anxious. I have gone to prepare a place for you. I'm going to come and receive you unto Myself."

Amazingly, we still enjoyed life and loved being with each other. I had loved Jim since the age of 15, but because of all we had been through together during the 52 years of our marriage, our love for each other had grown much deeper and more mature.

Jim knew how much I enjoyed going to the beach, so we found a house right on a private beach and spent a wonderful few days together. Jim often sat on the sun porch and just enjoyed watching the water and the sunsets. Once he went down to the water, saying "If you go in the water, I will." I replied, "You've got to be kidding." But the grin on his face meant he wasn't, so I jumped in with my clothes on. He threw his cane down, and went in too, pajamas and all.

We spent Thanksgiving with family, but we knew we would be home alone at Christmas. This was OK with both of us. Even though he was very weak, he somehow managed to get to the mall and find the things he always gave me for Christmas. There they were, under the tree, beautifully wrapped.

Jim had not been able to attend church very much for the past few months, but one Sunday in January he found the strength to get up and dress. He wanted us to go back to the church where my mother had belonged and join that church. The trip was more difficult than he had thought it would be, but he made it.

Some days were absolutely traumatic as Jim experienced pain that could not be stopped. Following one of these episodes, his doctors performed a surgery that gave him much relief from the pain. There were a few times when I felt anger at God for the pain Jim endured, but this emotion was fleeting.

As difficult as those days were, I praise God that Jim was able to win victory over several negative feelings he had harbored and he was able to go home free from them. He dealt with some lingering anger and bitterness toward other people and even toward God. These feelings had often stolen his joy and clouded his vision. One night Jim told me there was no one that he had not forgiven or that he felt bitterness toward.

As we recognized that our time together was probably getting shorter, our love for each other grew stronger. These were some of the most precious days of our life together.

During the next two months we were back and forth in the hospital. I stayed with him almost constantly. Finally, one morning, the doctors came one by one and told us, they could do no more. His internal medicine doctor said they would be sending him to a nursing home, but I firmly told him no. He then said he would help us set up a hospital bed in our home.

My sister, Ann, my two nieces, and Mary, who had been an immense help to us with housework and errands, had everything ready to go when we got home. Christin, my granddaughter, was coming from Mississippi to be with me. After a period of confusion that resulted from having too many doctors giving orders, we decided to call in Hospice.

Jim's sister, Caroline, came from Atlanta and I could hear them talking. Jim told her, "You know I'm going on a trip." When she asked where he was going, he replied, "To heaven. Where do you think I am going?" She asked how he was going? His odd reply was, "In a boat." He had told me several times in the last few weeks that he was getting ready to take a trip and reminded me of John 14:1-3, where Jesus promised His disciples that He was going to prepare a place for them and would come back and take them to be with Him.

Later that year I went in a little shop and my eyes fell on a plaque of a boat with a black Bible and a rose lying in the seat. The Scripture quote was "Come unto me all you that labor and I will give you rest." This reminded me of Jim's comment about going home in a boat. I purchased the plaque and always smile when I see it on my wall.

My Journey

Later he told me again in a very weak voice, "Shelvie, I'm getting ready to take the trip, and you can't go." I bent down and said, "Honey, you go on and don't worry about me. Go." With this, I released him to the Lord.

That evening Christin suggested that I try to get some sleep. She said she would stay with Jim during the night. I slept most of the night, but got up very early the next morning to check on them. I had just left Jim's room when the Hospice nurse called for me to come back quick and talk with him. Before I could say anything, I looked up. For a split second I actually saw an opaque cloud leaving his body. I knew that he was being carried by angels on a trip to be with his Lord.

Within minutes, my pastor and the music pastor were standing with me, offering to prayer for me. I wondered how they had gotten there so soon. The music pastor told me that God had impressed on him to stop by our house that morning. They came not knowing what had just happened. I was still in awe about what I had just witnessed, and I felt the need to praise and worship the Lord. For the next several minutes, I prayed and they prayed.

Hospice then called the funeral home to come and pick up Jim's body. While the director was there, he wanted to know if I would be coming to make arrangements later. My first thought was, "No! I can't do that." Then all of a sudden, I felt a renewed strength come. I left alone and told Ann and Christin where I was going, and asked them to come later. I went shopping with Christin for some clothes she could wear to the funeral. Then friends and relatives came from everywhere, bringing food, and offers of help, and comfort. In spite of being physically exhausted and grieving over the loss of my best friend, the sense of well-being and renewed strength continued.

Jim had wanted Al, his lifetime friend, to do his funeral along with our pastor. Al had become a gospel preacher. He recalled happy memories, Jim's love for family and friendships, and his strong faith in God. As I sat there listening to his words, I thought back over the years Jim and I had shared, treasuring the memories. Now his earthly journey had ended and he was living in a place that was free from the pains he had suffered.

Most of my immediate family had been taken home, and I knew I would someday see them all again. I was comforted by this thought in spite of the pain and grief of losing someone else I loved very much and facing an uncertain future.

It's hard to explain how someone can experience the deep pains of grief and at the same time be thankful for the past and have hope for the future. After Jim's death, some people expected me to fall apart emotionally, but amazingly I was able to continue with life unhindered by bitterness or anger or loneliness. I attribute this unexpected strength to how God honored Jim's many prayers for me, as well as God's promise to be my strength.

Week by week following Jim's funeral, there was evidence of God's care. My sister and I took a relaxing trip to Mrytle Beach. We went with several friends on a cruise to St. Thomas and St. Martin. When I decided to make some needed changes in the house, God sent a young Christian man who was just what I needed. Then Christin decided to move to Aiken and take a job here. She lived with me for several months, filling a deep need for companionship.

Grieving is a very personal thing, and there are no rules to follow. For me, I found it easier to continue with life when I could do things with family and friends. I also found that making a few changes in the house was a helpful thing to do. Above all, I found time to pray, read my Bible, and be in communion with my Heavenly Father.

Epilogue

As for the future, God has granted me some new and unexpected blessings. After renewing a friendship with an old friend I had known in the late 50's, Herschel L. Smith (Smitty) and I decided to marry. He has brought love, joy, fun, and security into my life.

One day Smitty commented about what a hard life I had lived. I had the privilege of telling him, "I've really had a wonderful life. I've known the unconditional love of a wonderful family. God has allowed me to experience His love, His strength, His joy, His steadfast presence, and eternal life. He has allowed me to teach His Word and to see the power of His Word change lives. I'm still learning to trust God, but I know He has a place and a purpose for me, as He does for each life."

Another unexpected blessing is Eason, a beautiful great grandson. I don't know what all the future holds, but I know it will be walked hand in hand with my Lord and Savior, Jesus.

Spiritual Victory

As Christians, we are all pilgrims in life on a journey that ultimately leads us home to heaven. During the journey, there will be wonderful mountain top experiences and there will be painful valleys to cross. When the journey becomes hard, it's easy to give up or become bitter or gravitate to things that are ultimately destructive. But, even in the most severe circumstances, we can choose to seek out God's truths and provisions and to respond by faith and obedience.

All of my questions were not answered and all of yours will not be, but I believe that God will give us enough insight to satisfy us as we continue on our journey. The secret things belong to God, but those things which are revealed belong to us and to our children. The secret things will be revealed in eternity where we will fully understand and continue to learn and praise God forever.

So, if you find yourself in a difficult situation, as I did, you may not understand what is really going on in your life. You may have been a faithful Christian, even a very active

Christian. You may feel like your whole world has come to an end or that God has forsaken you. Satan may be telling you all kind of lies about yourself or about God. You may consider yourself a complete failure. You may be so desperate as to feel that even God can't help you out of your situation.

To those Christian readers who relate to the things I have written about but still find themselves or their loved ones unable to deal their situations, I want to offer these thoughts. In order to grow and mature in our Christian walk, we must be sure that we have a firm grasp of foundational Truths.

One of the foremost things that God has chosen to reveal to us is that His love for us is unearned and unmerited. God taught me He really loved me and accepted me just like I was, faults and all. He even loved me before I knew Him as my Savior. I didn't have to do anything to earn His love. I just had to accept His gift of eternal life and His love for me. When the truth of His love for me finally became a reality, my life changed. I realized that if I never did another thing for my Lord, He would still love me, not for what I did, but for who I am—His child.

Salvation is through faith in Jesus alone. It is not the results of good works, traditions, or anything else other than Christ Himself. Jesus said, "...I am the way, the truth, and the life; no man cometh to the Father, but by Me." (John 14:6) God's holiness demands that we must be perfectly righteous in order to dwell in heaven with Him. Since this is impossible for anyone to do, our only hope is to put on the perfect righteousness that Jesus provides. When we recognize our own inability to ever be holy and righteous, we can accept His provision to be righteous in Jesus through faith.

As born again Christians our salvation is eternally secure. We should never allow doubts that our eternal life might be in jeopardy because we did something or failed to do something that displeased God. Our fellowship with God can be temporarily interrupted by sins, but He is always faithful to restore fellowship as we come to Him in repentance. Although we may temporarily lose our fellowship, we never lose our sonship and will always be His child. I John 5:11 says, "And this is the record, that God has given to us eternal life, and this life is in His Son…These things have I written unto you that believe on the name of the Son of God that you may know that you have eternal life."

Many people believe that we have to earn our salvation through obedience to a set of rules or requirements. This is known as legalism. A form of legalism tells us that in addition to possessing faith in Jesus, there are some other things we must do to keep our salvation. Legalism emphasizes self-righteousness and de-emphasizes the righteousness that comes through faith in our Lord Jesus. Legalism is full of pride in our own efforts as opposed to the meekness and humility that comes from faith in God's grace. In my case, strict church attendance, extreme modesty in dress, and avoiding alcohol and dancing were intertwined with the salvation experience. I was not sure what might happen if I failed to keep these rules, but I feared that it might somehow cause me to lose my salvation. Not being sure of my salvation was the inroad Satan used to plunge me into depression.

God's Word is Truth and Light and has the power to set us free from bondages. When the light of truth comes in, darkness goes out. Depression is based on lies and wrong thinking. We may believe lies about God or fail to realize that Satan brings darkness and depression. We should allow the Holy Spirit to help us find Truths in God's Word and to help us to correctly interpret Scripture. God's Word has the power to renew our minds.

Prayer is how we communicate with God. We enter into the very presence of God with praise and thanksgiving. There we can bring our petitions and requests to Him, share our disappointments with Him, ask for guidance and help, intercede for others, or just talk with Him. Jeremiah 33:3 says, "Call unto Me and I will answer you and show you great and mighty things that you know not." Philippians 4:6 tells us not to be anxious about anything, but let God know our requests, our feelings, our heart aches, our specific needs. When we talk to God about our situations, obey His Word, and trust Him to do as He says He will, then the peace of God, which passes all understanding, will guard our hearts and minds through Christ Jesus.

Forgiveness is essential for a Christian. We must receive forgiveness for our sins and we must forgive others for hurting or offending us. Know that God has provided a way through the cross in which our past, present, and future sins are forgiven. No matter what you have done God has assured you that you can have complete and absolute forgiveness if you come to Him in repentance. It was through the blood of Jesus

Christ that all our sins were paid once and for all according to Hebrews 10:10.

Unforgiveness towards others blocks healing. Ask the Holy Spirit of God to show you and bring to your mind anyone you have not forgiven. You may be harboring unforgiveness toward a mate, a mother, a father, friend, child, brother, sister, employer, or someone else. It could even be yourself or God. So, forgive those who have hurt or offended you. As we forgive, our Heavenly Father forgives us. (Matthew 6:14) If we do not forgive, Jesus says we will be turned over to the tormentors. (Matthew 18:34)

We must confess our sins, and not be overcome by past failures. Confess our sins. "If we confess our sins, He is faithful and just to forgive us of our sins and to cleanse us from all unrighteousness." (I John 1:9) Confession is to agree with God about what He calls sin and then to forsake those sins. No matter how huge your sins may appear and no matter what you have done, God has the power to forgive and cleanse you. Not only that, but God tells us in Joel 2:25, "I will restore to you the years the locust has eaten." Satan may continue to remind us of past sins, but by faith, we need to remember that God puts our sins under the blood of Jesus. He forgets them and remembers them no more.

In dealing with problems, we must commit them to God and trust Him. Commit everything to God. Sometimes we have to completely commit or surrender a problem in our life to God in order to find a solution. When you give a problem up to God, you can stop worrying about it and trust Him to work it out. Instead of dwelling on the problem, dwell on the solution and on God's sufficiency. There may be times when we don't get the answers we seek, but during those times, we need even more to trust Him. Romans 8:28 tells us that all things will work together for good to them that love God and for those who are called according to His purpose. Not everything that happens in life is good, but when we commit them to God, He can cause them to work together for good.

We need to understand that one of Satan's main tools is to accuse us of sins and failure, but that God desires to bless us with abundant life. If you find that negative depressive or accusing thoughts are constantly coming against you, you can know that they're not coming from God. The Bible refers to Satan as the accuser of the brethren. Respond to enemy attacks by remembering that Satan was defeated at the Cross and Jesus died to set us free from the bondage of sin. Memorize Romans 8:1 and speak these words directly to the accuser. "There is now therefore no condemnation to them which are in Christ Jesus..." Refuse to listen to negative thoughts or "voices" that tell you there is no hope, because this will take you deeper into depression and despair. I do not believe that it is God's will for someone to live in perpetual darkness because Jesus said He came to give us abundant life. Darkness and depression are not abundant life. The abundant life Jesus is talking about is an overcoming life, with love, joy, peace, and contentment.

Cultivate an optimistic, thankful attitude toward life. Both grief and depression can be lessened by cultivating an optimistic, thankful, hopeful attitude. Even in grief we can thank the Lord for our loved ones and the time we had with them.

We can find comfort in God and in His Word when experiencing grief and loss. Almost every hurt in life involves some kind of loss. Depression causes much loss and grief to many. The death of someone you love may be the biggest burden one will ever carry. Recovering from grief isn't a single event, but a process. After the loss of a loved one, you should ask God to direct your path. Grief will grip you suddenly, but let go slowly. As we heal slowly from a wound or surgery, so do our hearts after the death of a loved one.

God tells us to cast all our care on Him. Grief over your loved one is the greatest cares one may have to carry, but we do not have to carry it alone. Jesus bore our sorrows and carried our griefs. Ask your Heavenly Father for comfort. He knows what you're going through, because He is the God of all comfort. II Corinthians 1:3-4 says, "Blessed be God, even the Father of our Lord Jesus Christ, the Father of mercies, and the God of all comfort, who comforts us in all our tribulation that we may be able to comfort them who are in any trouble, by the comfort with which we ourselves are comforted of God."

During the healing process, crying is healthy. It is an emotional and physical release. Sometimes one may feel like they are going crazy. Everyday tasks can become difficult or demanding. During this time period it is good not to overexert yourself. Tell family and friends how you feel, and be patient with yourself.

How long grief lasts is different with everyone. Mental health experts advise those experiencing grief not making major changes the first year, but this may be different with everyone. I have found that there is a point in the grieving process when you are able to think of the deceased without pain. It doesn't imply that you won't miss the one you lost; it only means that your sadness will be different, gentler, and less wrenching.

We can be set free from depression through faith in God's Word. While we cannot control when we will be confronted with grief, we can reject depression and come against it with God's Word. We're never to lose sight of God's ability to handle any situation or storm that may arise. The awesome sovereignty and infinite love of God is revealed when He is able to take a desperate seemingly hopeless situation and turn it into a blessing.

Storms expose our weaknesses, increase our faith in and love for God. They can help us to become more like God intends us to be and can be the basis for many blessings to ourselves and to others. God has been able to use the storms of grief and depression to cleanse and rebuild many things in my life. They have enabled me to counsel and minister to others who see no hope and point them to a mighty God who can take any situation and remake it into a victory.

I am so thankful for the opportunity to share my story with you. My prayer is that God will use my story to encourage and challenge you in your journey.

There will always be times of weakness in your journey – at that time, turn your thoughts to Jesus, and you will sense the strength of the Holy Spirit. If you would like to receive all that Jesus has done for you and to make Him your Lord and Savior, pray this prayer:

Dear Lord Jesus, I am a sinner. I ask you to forgive my sins and I receive you as my Lord and Savior. I believe you died, were buried, and rose again. Thank you for forgiving me and giving me eternal life and filling my heart with your love, peace, and joy. – Amen

My prayer is that God will use my story to encourage and challenge you in your journey.

SDG